1. Leveling up your craft to write a story that lives long after you've left the planet is what some might call a ridiculous goal.

2. You know that you will not tell that story after reading just one how-to-write book.

3. You know that you will not tell that story as the result of taking one seminar.

4. You know that creating a timeless work of art will require the dedication of a world-class athlete. You will be training your mind with as much ferocity and single-minded purpose as an Olympic gold medal hopeful. That kind of cognitive regimen excites you, but you just haven't found a convincing storytelling dojo to do that work.

5. The path to leveling up your creative craft is a dark and treacherous course. You've been at it a long time, and it often feels like you're wearing three-dimensional horse blinders. More times than you'd wish to admit, you're not sure if you are moving north or south or east or west. And the worst part? You can't see anyone else, anywhere going through what you're going through. You're all alone.

WELCOME TO THE STORY GRID UNIVERSE

1. We believe we find meaning in the pursuit of creations that last longer than we do. This is *not* ridiculous. Seizing opportunities and overcoming obstacles as we stretch ourselves to reach for seemingly unreachable creations is transformational. We believe this pursuit is the most valuable and honorable way to spend our time here. Even if—especially if—we never reach our lofty creative goals.

2. Writing just one story isn't going to take us to the top. We're moving from point A to Point A^{5000}. We've got lots of mountains to climb, lots of rivers and oceans to cross, and many deep dark forests to traverse along the way. We need topographic guides, and if they're not available, we'll have to figure out how to write them ourselves.

3. We're drawn to seminars to consume the imparted wisdom of an icon in the arena, but we leave with something far more valuable than the curriculum. We get to meet the universe's other pilgrims and compare notes on the terrain.

4. The Story Grid Universe has a virtual Dojo, a university in which to work out and get stronger—a place to stumble, correct mistakes, and stumble again, until the moves become automatic and mesmerizing to outside observers.

5. The Story Grid Universe has a performance space, a publishing house dedicated to leveling up the craft with clear boundaries of progress, and the ancillary reference resources to pack for each project mission. There is an infinite number of paths to where you want to be, with a story that works. Seeing how others have made it down their own yellow-brick roads to release their creations into the timeless creative cosmos will help keep you on the straight and narrow path.

All are welcome—the more, the merrier. But please abide by the golden rule:

Put the work above all else, and trust the process.

ACTION STORY

THE PRIMAL GENRE

SHAWN COYNE

STORY GRID

STORY GRID

Story Grid Publishing LLC
223 Egremont Plain Road
PMB 191
Egremont, MA 01230

First Story Grid Publishing Paperback Edition April 2020

For Information about Special Discounts for Bulk
Purchases, please visit www.storygridpublishing.com

ISBN: 978-1-64501-013-5
Ebook: 978-1-64501-014-2

For

All Past, Present, and Future Story Nerds

ABOUT THIS BOOK

Action Story: The Primal Genre explores the fundamental constraints and patterns of the action genre, where all great storytelling begins. Our aim is to jump-start beginning writers and refresh professionals on the fundamentals of what we view as the first and most essential kind of story.

We identify and analyze twelve *content genres* in our Story Grid methodology. We know one from the other because each has its particular characteristics and straightforward forces of conflict at play. The *Action genre* is one of nine *external genres* (Action, War, Horror, Crime, Thriller, Western, Love, Performance, and Society) that are driven primarily by external conflicts between humans, between humans and nature, or between humans and supernatural monsters or forces. Three *internal genres* (Status, Worldview, and Morality) explore conflicts within individuals.

This book includes a 20-point game plan showing how the classic Action Story moves forward on the ground, from beginning to end. We break Action Story into four quarters. In each quarter, we find the critical events of the action genre in Story Grid's Five Commandments of Storytelling—Inciting Incident, Progressive Complications (especially the Turning Point Complication), Crisis, Climax, and Resolution.

WHAT YOU NEED TO KNOW TO GET STARTED

We at Story Grid are dedicated to examining our work and the work of others scientifically, through multiple lenses. Over time, we refine and polish these lenses to create the highest resolution possible. While we are confident in the propositions we present here, we also know that our thinking keeps evolving as we adapt and integrate new information from the writers and editors in our growing community. Before you accept and employ our methods, you should weigh and analyze each of our statements yourself. Do the ideas make sense to you? Are you willing to test them carefully in your own writing and the works of authors you love? Will you contribute to clarifying and refreshing them?

We invite you to join us in exploring the multifaceted craft of storytelling, the means of expression that makes us human.

1

THE PRIMACY OF ACTION STORIES

A brush with death changes our lives.

We can have one of two psychological responses to a life-or-death event. We might come away from the trauma with the realization that we're not living up to our potential. Perhaps since childhood we have had beautiful dreams of creating something that epitomizes who we are and what we stand for, something unique that only we could imagine or execute. After a near-death experience, we put these dreams at the top of our list of priorities and pledge to fulfill them.

On the other hand, we might come face-to-face with death and conclude that we are not fully living, enjoying the everyday wonders of the world. Maybe we have been so goal-oriented that we haven't been able to appreciate a moment hanging out at a coffee shop with a friend or watching an old movie with our kids on a rainy Sunday afternoon. We resolve to slow down and take life as it comes, living mindfully in every moment.

Both of these responses are meaningful. When we have a run-in with something that's ultimately unknowable, like the experience of death, we are confronted by what philosophers call the *noumenal world.* It's hard for us to make sense of that world because we deal with everything based on the *phenomenal world* that we connect with through our senses and our minds. When we confront unknowable death, we respond with a focus on these two fundamental truths of life:

1. We have limited time to create something lasting, something that can contribute to the greater collective unconscious of our species.
2. We must pay attention to the moment-by-moment revelatory beauty inherent in the world around us.

Both mindsets are indispensable to our lives as humans, even if that's somewhat paradoxical.

Our struggle to integrate these two quests is at the heart action stories. We want to contribute to something greater than ourselves, *and* we want to stop striving and take life as it comes. While we often consider action stories to be a guilty pleasure because many are heavy on spectacle and less concerned with the deeper meaning of life and death, these stories are *primal and important.* Action stories are cross-cultural connectors. Every person on the planet understands the power of a great action story, no matter the language we speak or how we or the creators identify in terms of gender, race, religion, or other cultural categories.

As a thought experiment, let's look at action stories through one of Story Grid's favorite parlor games. What if tomorrow you forgot everything you've ever known about storytelling? What would you do? Where would you begin to relearn your craft?

Of course, barring some highly improbable blunt-force trauma to our noggins, we're not going to lose everything we know about story structure overnight. But it could be highly instructive to use our imaginations to consider what we would do if as storytellers our worst nightmare happened.

For anyone who has played competitive sports, having to start all over again is not unusual. The longer you participate in athletics, the more likely you are to find yourself injured and having to relearn your skills.

The soccer player who blows out one knee's anterior cruciate ligament on the field on a Friday faces unavoidable surgery on Monday. And that unnerving experience is soon followed by one of the most dreaded and painful words in the English language—rehab.

Rehab is a process of managing pain in the service of regaining fundamental skills. It doesn't just require an acceptance of intense discomfort. It involves abandoning our reliance on the practically unconscious mastery we've probably taken for granted.

In rehab, you have to relearn how to stand before you can walk. You have to relearn how to walk before you can jog. And it would be best if you jogged before you tried to run. Then you have to relearn what muscles must be rebuilt to change direction. That's when the real pain begins—when you are ninety percent back to form. The last ten percent is what separates your skills from everyone else's, and so they are the most difficult to regenerate. Now you have to learn how to be yourself again.

Relearning or rehabbing any skill— including writing—is a humbling process, but it's not baffling.

You do what you need to do to stand. You

do what you need to do to walk. You do what you need to do to jog. You do what you need to do to run. You do what you need to do to change direction. Repeat. Those are the five essential stages of rebuilding a knee.

Now we're back to our parlor game: What would be the series of intellectual steps necessary to relearn or refresh our storytelling skills? What must we do to *stand* as storytellers?

Good old Roman emperor and philosopher Marcus Aurelius recommended we peel back the onion layers of a skill, which is an excellent place to start. He suggests, "Of each particular thing ask: What is it in itself? What is its nature?"

Those who've read anything by Story Gridders will not be surprised by our starting point in understanding what story is "in itself. We examine story through genres.

Let's now take the first step in our storytelling rehab. To answer the question about story's nature, we should probably go back to the beginning and ask simply: Where did stories come from?

2

WHERE STORIES CAME FROM

How did we *Homo sapiens* survive in a hostile environment more than 300,000 years ago when we first began to thrive on Earth?

The emergence of our ability to tell stories exponentially increased our adaptive advantage. Narrative was the critical psychotechnology—a tool that came from our conscious minds—that allowed knowledge to spread between individuals and to carry forward from generation to generation.

Sometime back in the Stone Age, connection and communication between individuals enabled us to adapt far faster to our environment than any other species. Stories—in the form of cave paintings, songs, sculptures, and eventually formal language— made humans more formidable together than alone. If I know something that will save your life and I share that knowledge with you, together we become a force of two that can survive longer than either of us could alone. In this case, one plus one does not equal two. The power of two people working together is far greater than the sum of the two working alone.

And the way we work together is through storytelling.

Stories give us advantages in survival, and that spreads exponentially. They prepare us for the unexpected. Random events will drop into our lives at any moment, challenging our abilities to process and adapt to them. Stories help teach us not to panic when the unexpected happens.

When the unexpected does occur, we can search our story-memory banks and find a way to model our behavior to our best advantage. Stories tell us how we might get what we want and need by mimicking how a character in a book (whether fictional or real) got what they wanted and needed. Stories also teach us how to avoid the behavior of those who failed to obtain their heart's desire. Stories are collective knowledge storage tanks, and what's more, there is no limit to their size. Abundance is built into the system, and we all drink from and refill the same tank.

The shared knowledge stories give us can provide quick practical information or profound existential answers to help us solve the most severe problems we face.

Just think of asking a friend for advice about how they learned a particular skill. Unconsciously, you ask because you're collecting possible options you could act on to learn what they know. You're building a story-memory bank in your own mind for that particular want or need. What better way than to see if a similar story has been created before we plunge into the darkness?

Your friend may respond with: "When I first set out to learn how to _____, I _____," and off they'll go with a detailed description of how they faced many roadblocks, but ultimately, their ambition to learn the skill triumphed. The success story they tell you will serve as a *prescriptive tale*, modeling your behavior on your journey to achieve what they already possess.

On the other hand, when we hear stories of failure, they serve as *cautionary tales* for avoiding the behavior that led to dissatisfaction or disaster.

We use stories to model our behavior, as frames of reference to compare and contrast how we're doing in life's great journey. If that's true, what might have been the first story ever shared? Wouldn't it have responded to an essential want and need that we all share?

What is that universal want and need?

It's pretty simple. We all want and need to survive, to stay alive. Action stories give us myriad ways by which we can effectively survive the unexpected. That is why we find them so compelling.

Action stories were the first stories because they offered specific advantages for our survival, teaching us how to overcome life-threatening external forces, such as avoiding a pack of hungry wolves or surviving a snowstorm.

The stakes for action stories are at the outer limits of normal experience, showing us brushes with death. And because the line between life and death is so tenuous in the telling, we can't help but pay attention to these stories. We lock into them as if we were facing the plot circumstances ourselves.

Ancient cave drawings prove how important these stories were to our loincloth-clad forebears. Securing water, food, and shelter was critical to our survival, and the behavioral prescriptions that helped us get those survival needs met were the most important to communicate. A quick glance at any cave painting will reveal that the first shared stories were about *how to hunt or gather food*. This illustrates how our metaphysical toolbox serves our physical needs.

Our bodies attune our minds to the natural world first with our five senses and the feelings they generate. Then our minds must make sense of those feelings, figure out what they mean, and then prescribe a series of motor actions that adapt our bodies to the reality of the natural world. It's a dynamic system.

Our bodies tell us we're cold, and our minds respond by telling us to walk to the closet and put on a sweater.

This coupling of our minds and bodies is why the Story Grid community works diligently to link our investigation of storytelling to natural phenomena catalogued and analyzed by science. We maintain that stories can be investigated with science, and there is a clear link between story and other investigative scientific disciplines, primarily holistic cognitive science.

Science is about categorizing phenomena, understanding what induces the phenomena to emerge, and then figuring out a way to cause it to occur on demand. As writers, we all wish to cause effects, and the science of story can help us.

In other words, Story Grid is about causing the effect of a working, cathartic story by analyzing it scientifically.

Because stories are psychotechnologies, or mind tools, that give human beings adaptive advantages in contending with unexpected environmental change, they are indispensable to us as we navigate the complex natural environment. They help us get what we need in the face of unexpected conflict. They warn us about and teach us how to handle an unexpected event before it happens to us and how to metabolize it after it's happened.

We believe that each genre content story category is associated with satisfying a different kind of fundamental human need. And our twelve genre content categories map onto Abraham Maslow's schematic representation of humans' psychological needs to provide a starting point. For a deeper dive into this relationship, visit https://storygrid.com/beats/action.

The primal human need above all others is *survival*. If we can't stay alive, then everything else we may need or want isn't going to matter.

Action stories are so compelling because they focus on our need to survive. In fact, they form the on-the-ground narrative for every story ever told. They address head-on the problem of staying alive when forces beyond our control threaten our very existence.

So, let's go back and now directly answer Marcus Aurelius's questions applied to an action story: "*What is it in itself? What is its nature?*"

An action story is *a tool to help us survive unexpected external changes in our environment.* That is its essence.

As writers, when we get stuck while creating an action story, we need to go back to that core definition. Action stories are *prescriptive tales for survival* or *cautionary tales about behaviors that will lead to premature death.*

Emerson stared out an ominous sea while she contemplated possibly having just six months left to live.

The idea weighed on her like an iron cloak...

3

THE CORE LIFE VALUE OF ACTION STORY

Action Story, which is how we will refer to the action genre from here on, is all about a character's or characters' movement along the universal life–to–death *value spectrum*. We sometimes call this a *polarity shift*.

Each scene in Action Story takes the protagonist closer to, or further away from, staying alive. While the majority of scenes will also have unique micro value shifts embedded within them, such as alone–together or excited–despairing, the result of every scene can be evaluated at the on-the-ground life–death level too. Again, the question we must ask is: Is the character closer to or further away from death on the value spectrum at the end of the scene?

First let's clarify what we mean by "value."

A value is each person's rule of thumb about whether something is meaningful. Does the change in their condition make life more meaningful and good or more meaningless and bad?

Although each person's set of values is different, there are some universal values with which we all generally agree.

We inherently value life, safety, justice, love, truth, respect, and courage. Our interpretations of these values fall along a *value spectrum* and are context-driven. But generally, most people would agree that our lives are more meaningful in the pursuit of such positive shared values. When we move closer to a purer form of justice, for example, we find that experience pleasant and meaningful. When we drift further away from our ideal definition, we see the experience as unpleasant and meaningless.

Action Story's primary value is life. Every scene in the story should have a polarity shift that moves a character between varying degrees of the life value.

The question to ask when evaluating any action scene is: "Does the scene move the character closer to life or to death?" Tracking the movement of this global value on a Story Grid graph will generate the arc of the action story and is a clear way for you to see if the narrative is varied and compelling.

Now let's clarify what we mean by value

spectrum. Take a look at the Life–Death Value Spectrum graphic below.

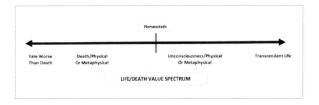

The line to the right of the word "homeostatic" represents life in all its existential nuances, while the line to the left represents approaching death. At the far end of the positive side, *transcendent life* means creating a legacy of behavior worthy of emulation, both in our lifetime and after our death—in other words, attaining metaphorical immortality. And, yes, there is a "fate worse than death," which is metaphorical damnation and is equal to but the opposite of transcendence. Damnation is the result of a life so reprehensible that it defines how *not* to be.

Consider a situation in which death would be merciful, when someone is in such torment that to lose their life would be a relief. That torment could be physical (the body is incapable of sensing anything other than pain) or metaphysical (the mind is in such a state of such distress that it is confronting the darkest components of the universe).

While the fate worse than death, or damnation, value is essential to establish in the horror and thriller genres, it is not always necessary to bring it into play explicitly in Action Story. The reader should be able to intuit this most extreme negative value from the context of the story, without putting it onstage in Action Story's events and without having the characters experience it.

The spectrum of life–to–death values includes many different expressions—far more than just the five we've placed on the graphic. When we're not feeling 100 percent because we have the flu, we're certainly alive, but not living at the most positive end of the life value. Similarly, if we accidentally veer off of the road while driving and approach a cliff that drops a thousand feet into the sea, we may be perilously close to death, but haven't gone over the edge yet. You can see that there are innumerable variations on being close to life or close to death. The imaginative ways that storytellers play with these variations and nuances make Action Story compelling.

We represent this state of being changing through time in every scene of a story using a value spectrum, with the negative end on the left and the positive end on the right.

For example, a scene about whether or not the protagonist can convince the guardian of a building to let her inside will be about the tools the protagonist uses to convince the guardian to do what she wants. This particular scene will shift from the value of unconvincing–to–convincing or perhaps, outside–to–inside. But it will *also* shift on the global life–death value spectrum because if the protagonist does not gain admittance to the building she will find herself closer to death.

It's essential to understand that scenes often turn on multiple life values. But the trick is to make sure that as you're writing you choose *one value* to focus on as the one that shifts in your scene and stick to it. Other value shifts will emerge from that concentrated effort, and your reader will intuit them naturally.

If you're writing an action story, you will need to check that the value choice you've made also has the overarching life–death value shift embedded in it. Otherwise, even if other aspects of the scene are terrific, it won't feel right to the reader. It won't fall within the action story category, and thus, will confuse and ultimately disappoint your readers.

To go back to the example of the character trying to gain admittance to a building, the successful movement from unconvincing–to–convincing will increase the probability that she will live to see another day. So, this scene has a *micro value movement* of unconvincing–to– convincing and a *macro value movement* of closer-to-death–to–closer-to-life.

Keep in mind that it's best not to overwhelm yourself evaluating micro and macro values simultaneously. As you edit your work, focus on just one of these levels of analysis (use one lens) at a time. We call this skill "shifting levels of analysis," which means that you move from the overarching big-picture (the universal life–death value) to the microscopic view (the scene-specific value) and back again. In other words, you engage in a top-down macro analysis and a bottom-up micro analysis, but you do them separately.

It's always worth reminding yourself of this rule: *Don't even think about these editorial tools while you are writing.* Allow your inner storyteller to drive your drafts, not your outer editor. Again, commit to one level of analysis at a time.

Some questions to include in your analysis are: Do the scene and the global story align? Do they work together? Or are they at odds?

If the scene does not have a shift in the global value at stake, revise it so that it does. If the universal value at stake doesn't serve your most indispensable scene, consider a different global value shift and whether you need to switch genres.

To sum it all up: Value shifts are critical components of any story and must be present at every level of its construction. Values are what change from the beginning to the end of the scene and from the beginning of the story to the end of the story.

4

ACTION STORY'S CONTROLLING IDEA

Let's go back to Marcus Aurelius's first principles and ask, "What is the purpose of a story?" Writer Joan Didion's view may help us:

"We tell ourselves stories in order to live...We look for the sermon in the suicide, for the social or moral lesson in the murder of five. We interpret what we see, select the most workable of the multiple choices. We live entirely, especially if we are writers, by the imposition of a narrative line upon disparate images, by the 'ideas' with which we have learned to freeze the shifting phantasmagoria which is our actual experience."
— Joan Didion, *The White Album*

"The imposition of a narrative line upon

disparate images" is the storyteller's job, whether they're making sense of a documented real-life event in a work of nonfiction or creating a fictional event modeled on real-life experiences. Stories are sense-making tools that help us metabolize and integrate unexpected changes in our lives (at Story Grid, we call these unexpected changes *pheres*). They make events meaningful.

When something makes sense to us—when we know the rules—we're able to act accordingly. For example, if we know that the object of a particular game is to get a ball into a goal without using our hands, we can make sense of playing a soccer match.

So, the controlling idea of the story of soccer is "Within the defined arena, without players using their hands, the winning team will get more balls in the goal than their opponent." That statement is the controlling idea of every story about soccer ever written. The story of soccer can only happen under particular *constraints*, including the rules of the game and the defined arena.

Controlling ideas are the boiled-down *lessons* of story, the embedded knowledge inside of the entertainment. Stories don't just include controlling ideas—these are the very purpose, the message we take away at the end, whether we realize it or not. And they stay inside us too, directing how we make sense of what Didion calls our "shifting phantasmagoria" of real-life experience.

What else can we say about controlling ideas? We could divide them into categories:

1. Positive Prescriptions: "To win, kick the ball across the goal line more times than your opponent."
2. Negative Cautions: "If you don't kick the ball across the goal line more times than your opponent, you'll lose."

It would seem that every story has just two possible abstract outcomes. The character either adapts to and integrates a change event into their life history and finds the meaning of that event *positive*, or they fail to adapt to and integrate the change event and find the meaning of that event *negative*. And depending on the storyteller's choices, the reader, listener, or viewer will learn how to make sense of their own life experiences by using the story as a frame of reference.

We map a new story onto our own life's phantasmagoria in such a way that it helps us make sense of our lives. And when we make sense of our lives, we can make meaning; and when we make meaning, we can make choices and adapt to change. Making sense of incoming perceptions fires our meaning-making machinery, creating a binary choice. Our choices lead to actions that cause effects in our environment.

Now let's consider the specifics of controlling ideas in Action Story.

Because action stories are so primal, they always have an embedded global prescriptive or cautionary life lesson showing us how to survive. This fundamental lesson is a cause and effect relationship that can be boiled down to a single sentence. Many storytellers and editors use the word "theme" instead of "controlling idea." When you hear writers talk about themes, they are usually referencing the takeaways or messages in their stories.

Story Grid has adopted the clear and specific approach that story thinker Robert McKee uses to define controlling ideas. Our interpretation of McKee's definition includes three components:

1. A controlling idea must be boiled down to the fewest possible words and no longer than one-sentence.
2. The idea must describe the climactic value change of the entire story, whether positive or negative.
3. The idea must specifically discuss

the cause of the value shift (the effect).

In other words, a story makes sense to us when its unexpected cause creates an effect that results in a prescriptive behavior to model or a cautionary behavior to avoid. What would be Action Story's two kinds of global controlling ideas?

A Prescriptive Action Story Controlling Idea: Survival requires the protagonist to insightfully outwit or overpower mortal threats from an unexpected environmental change, unexpected lethal threats from another person or group, or both.

A Cautionary Action Story Controlling Idea: Death results when the protagonist fails to have the insight necessary to overpower or outwit mortal threats from an unexpected environmental change, unexpected threats from another person or group, or both.

Most action stories that we find masterful or guilty pleasures fall in the prescriptive category. Why?

We have certain expectations of stories about life and death. We expect to feel better about facing our mortality after experiencing them. So, unconsciously, our desire to arm ourselves with new ideas about the indomitable human spirit motivates us to engage with Action Story. We want to be inspired by heroic deeds from extraordinary (and ordinary) beings facing seemingly impossible-to-overcome circumstances.

If we part with hours of our time concentrating on a storyteller's creation and then walk away with the confirmation that we're fallible and incapable of holding back death, we may not think of that as time well spent.

To put it another way: If the protagonist dies in the end, it's a bummer.

Does this mean that every action story has to end happily ever after?

Of course not.

But death at the end of an action story has to be meaningful to satisfy the audience. The protagonist has to die for a reason. They must sacrifice themselves for the benefit of those they leave behind, the survivors. Why?

All of us need to be both self-reliant and capable of conforming and integrating into a larger group. This pull between putting ourselves first and putting the group first has evolved over hundreds of thousands of years. Optimal attunement to *both* necessities is evolution's recipe for survival. Taking care of one's personal primal needs first and then taking part in a cooperative, synergistic, and trusted group is the path to a meaningful life.

If your story's protagonist perishes in the service of a greater good, that action reinforces a core truth that we all inherently understand. If someone can leave Earth providing an example of a life well lived and in the service of those who remain, it is deeply meaningful.

If there is no sacrificial component to a protagonist's death, the audience despairs. They despair because the takeaway from the experience is the idea that life is meaningless, that human beings have no purpose on the planet. Does all that we've sensed, felt, thought, and enacted amount to nothing?

You may believe in a postmodern ideology that argues life is random, meaningless, and relative, and you may want to represent that worldview in a story. You may have profound reasons for writing a story with the takeaway that "life is meaningless," but what we at Story Grid suggest is that that kind of story will not work. At least, it will not work under our definition of "work."

Let's pause to define stories that *work*.

We believe a story that works is a story that satisfies readers so much that they share it and recommend it to others so that it has the possibility of transcending time. A story that transcends time, like *Pride and Prejudice*, is read and loved even when the creator is no longer living. That's the pinnacle of story creation in our Story Grid world—the thing we all hope to achieve one day.

It may be true that there is no purpose to human endeavors on Earth. Perhaps a random series of coincidences led to our evolution here, and eventually, we're all going to die because our behavior will lead to the destruction of our entire ecosystem. If that is true, whether or not your story works according to our definition doesn't matter anyway.

And maybe your story of human life's meaninglessness will work for you and an audience of like-minded nihilists. We still suggest it won't work through time.

Hmm. Let's leave it at that, and return to writing an *innovative* action story.

If stories that put forward prescriptive models of behavior result in the same old ending (the protagonist's triumph), and cautionary tales without meaningful sacrifice result in meaningless death (the protagonist's choices fail to defeat overwhelming forces), what's an aspiring Action Story writer to do?

Some writers focus on spectacle. They create innovative fight or chase sequences that readers, listeners, and viewers have not experienced before. Sometimes, these volatile movements distract us enough to forget about deriving meaning from the story, and we fall in love with the blur of motion. We've all experienced these kinds of stories. We even enjoy them to a degree.

But these stories are the equivalent of fast food. Our moment-to-moment experience inside of them is compelling, but there is no nutritional value to the meal.

Is there a way to create spectacular active movement in a story and also embed a meaningful message?

Yes.

There is a third variety of controlling idea for Action Story related to Story Grid's conception of a cognitive science-based *meta-myth* that encompasses all of the more narrowly defined messages of each of our specific content genre definitions. Let's look at this third option in more detail. But first, we should describe that meta-myth behind all the stories we find most meaningful.

The Transcendent Story Grid Controlling Idea

We gain meaning when we self-actualize and actively pursue our individual primary concern through exploratory being, growing, and creating over time.

Geez. That's pretty abstract and a lot to digest.

Another way of putting it is that we simply need to figure out *who we are* and what we should be doing here on Earth, and then do that thing as a way of serving the rest of our ecosystem. For example, Story Grid community members have a primary concern focused on exploring the wonder of storytelling. So that's what drives our growth and our creations.

This transcendent controlling idea has to be quite abstract because we're attempting to boil down the essence of a vast pot of disparate stories. Keep in mind, too, that this idea is a Story Grid conception based on our desire to align story theory with the exploratory findings of cognitive science. We will parse out this entire paradigm in future projects, but for now, let's look at the implications of this controlling idea for Action Story only. We can translate the idea into language that is about Action Story's pursuit of survival.

The Transcendent Story Grid Controlling Idea for Action Story

The meaning of life and death reveals itself when, in pursuit of survival, the protagonist learns to sacrifice themselves in the service of their fellow human beings' survival and creative growth.

In practical terms, if the protagonist dies, they must do so sacrificially so that others gain the power to transform their potential into creation through their own agency. This third variety of controlling idea is the message underneath a compelling action story that does not end with the protagonist's external triumph.

Can you see how stories with negative, less-than-triumphant endings can have prescriptive messages embedded inside what appear to be cautionary tales? Integrating this dynamism is the master storyteller's challenge.

5

ACTION STORY'S SELECTIVE CONVENTIONS

Conventions are essential concepts writers should understand and apply to all stories of a particular genre. They constrain the story and give it boundaries.

Remember that stories are simulations of life and that life occurs in all sorts of domains. These domains are the particular arenas in which we agents (the people trying to get what we want and need) apply our agency to cause a change or effect.

We write causes that create effects. That's what we do.

We're hungry (sustenance domain), so we cook something (cause) to effect a change (no longer hungry). We actualize our choice by eating what we cook and thus satisfy a sustenance domain need.

We live in extraordinarily *complex*

environments. They're so complex that we may be incapable of approaching an understanding of just how intricately structured they are. But we try to do so anyway.

We do this by creating *complicated* systems. Complicated systems allow us to follow specific step-by-step procedures in such a way that we can cause an effect with certainty. If you want an apple, and it is being sold for a dollar, you can use a dollar that you have earned doing other things or borrow it from someone else to cause the desired effect. You hand over the dollar (cause), and you get the apple (effect).

We take that indispensable system for granted today. But thousands of years ago, trading with someone else to meet your needs and wants was a big problem. Until we figured out how to create a mode of exchange (money), getting an apple from someone willing to part with one was difficult.

The psychotechnology that solved the trading problem was figuring out how to constrain all of the innumerable approaches to the problem. By creating a brand-new *metaphor* for valuable things and labeling it *money*, then getting everyone to accept that constraint, we created a system to make sense out of the complexities, finding a way to work with each other to the best advantage of everyone.

There are two kinds of story constraints.

We have *selective constraints* that narrow a big problem into a solvable search space. And we have *enabling constraints* that give rise to possible solutions to the big problem.

Selective constraints funnel the problem into a specific category, a need-based domain. And enabling constraints inside that particular domain give rise to the causes necessary to achieve specific effects.

Let's begin our exploration of Action Story's conventions by focusing on its selective constraints, the ones that narrow the problem domain. Remember that Action Story sets out to explore the life–death spectrum of values. So, we'll need to identify the kinds of environments, also known as the settings, that give rise to life-or-death conflicts.

THE SETTING

The setting of Action Story is critical because it determines the quality of the events that occur on stage. While there are limitless settings to choose from, the fictional world you are creating has to have some specific abstract qualities to serve as the ecosystem that will believably give rise to intense, primal life-or-death conflicts.

A disturbed, unbalanced physical and social environment gives rise to conflict.

The world you present at the beginning of your action story cannot be a perfectly harmonious system. If everyone is precisely integrated into its social structure and has their primal needs provided for, you will have difficulty getting an audience to suspend their disbelief. No matter how satisfied any of us may be, we're very good at finding imbalances in other life domains. Very rarely do we feel at one with our entire ecosystem.

What is required in Action Story is a beneath-the-surface asymmetry. That is, there should be a bubbling sense among the characters on the page (and within the audience's mind) that something negative is about to happen, that conflicting worldviews are about to clash.

To take a traditional example, realistic action stories written during the Cold War all had a primal disturbance at the core of their setting. The fate of the planet rested on maintaining a delicate balance of power between the United States and the Soviet Union. So the action stories that came out of this era concerned a destabilization of that balance and the efforts necessary to restore it to equilibrium.

In a more recent story such as *127 Hours* (the movie adaptation of Aron Ralston's memoir *Between a Rock and a Hard Place*), the audience knows there is a genuine danger beneath the surface of the environment. This story begins with the protagonist enjoying a beautiful day in the desert. But the audience knows there are many asymmetries of power inherent in that ecosystem. People in the desert could make a small mistake and suffer severe consequences. They are at the mercy of a harsh, indifferent environment that could snuff out their lives at any moment. This is the primal environment we all inhabit, no matter how secure we may feel at any particular time.

The setting you choose, whether it's a dystopian future in a book like Tim Grahl's *The Threshing* or a high-rise office building as in the film *Die Hard*, must include complex *asymmetries of power* that give rise to unexpected events.

Dueling Hierarchies

A core tool of Story Grid is our hierarchy lens, which you can use to pinpoint conflict opportunities within a setting, revealing where and how you might embed power asymmetry.

There are two kinds of hierarchies. The first is what we call the **Growth Hierarchy**. Growing up is a series of progressive cognitive leaps we make from the moment we're born until the moment we die. It's how we become more adaptive versions of ourselves, with ever-higher skills and capabilities.

Becoming requires *agency*, the ability to choose an action and enact it.

The growth hierarchy ascension requires two additional components: 1) the rise of an inspiring salience, or something that becomes extraordinarily relevant and resonant to us, and 2) help from other people.

To become a classical music appreciator or a Civil War buff you need someone to emulate. We all seek mentors and their works to guide us to the actualization of our aims. If we wish to master a skill, we look for advice from those who have already mastered that skill. We then model our behavior on those masters, and step-by-step, we climb up the skills hierarchy to become better and better craftspeople. The growth hierarchy is a human phenomenon that allows our species to develop and survive in ways that serve the individual and ideally, the greater society—unless the growth choice is to become the best destroyer of worlds rather than a creator of worlds.

The growth hierarchy is the sense-making and meaning-making system that keeps us on a path of progress, and it is responsible for our ever-increasing ways of improving our cognition. It is how we align ourselves with truth and embed ourselves in metaphysical reality.

Climbing the creative growth hierarchy is,

in Story Grid terms, the thematic and climactic way of the *luminary agent*, or protagonist (in gendered terms, the hero or heroine). We'll look at more about the luminary agent shortly.

The second kind of hierarchy is the **Power/Dominance Hierarchy**. Power is what we usually think of when we hear the word "hierarchy." The power/dominance hierarchy has nothing to do with growth or becoming. It is merely a pyramid built on status and domination of others. It is the structure by which people, through earned or unearned power, deprive others of agency. For example, a mentor dominates and belittles an apprentice to keep the apprentice from surpassing them. Or a leader with few skills beyond coercion and manipulation dominates an institution.

The *shadow agent* is the antagonist to the *luminary agent,* or protagonist. The shadow agent is the brilliant intellectual force that wants to strictly order the world according to their ideology, to reach the top of the power pyramid and control those beneath. The way of the shadow agent is to claw to the top of the power/dominance hierarchy and rule the lesser beings beneath by robbing them of their agency or coercing them to give up their agencies.

These hierarchies are not necessarily

horrific black or white conditions. We don't live in pure growth systems, nor do we live in pure power systems. There are elements of both in every social construct. Only in the extremes do we find real malevolence.

Isaiah Berlin famously considered the difficulties in managing democratic agency in a seminal 1958 lecture at Oxford, "Two Concepts of Liberty," an investigation that still provides valuable context to contemporary world events.

Many power/dominance hierarchies work, and many people find comfort in their positions within those hierarchies. Plenty of CEOs, political leaders, mothers, and fathers hold their places with humility and do their best to encourage others to grow. Those beneath the CEO recognize the skill sets of the leaders above them as more comprehensive than their own and understand that those who are more experienced and knowledgeable should have the final say in executive decisions.

Some enlightened leaders have risen to the top of hierarchies and used their power creatively to encourage growth in those less powerful. Marcus Aurelius was one such leader, stressing growth for the individual and controlled order for the masses.

Like most things we do at Story Grid, we view the hierarchical framework not as either/or but as a spectrum of values. A tyrannical power/dominance hierarchy sits on one end of the spectrum and a pure transcendent kind of growth hierarchy on the other.

By using the hierarchy lens when creating your setting, you can position your fictional world along this spectrum and think through the changes that might occur to move the political disposition of the environment one way or the other.

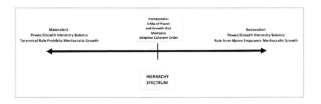

The two poles of this spectrum are the first consideration.

A pure power/dominance hierarchy is one in which there is a central authority figure or star chamber of members. What they decide is the gospel; all those beneath them must abide by their dictates. All citizens of that world must turn over their agency. Any who question the omnipotence of the authority figure are cast out, punished, incarcerated, or killed. Tyranny is not adaptive to changes in its environment and is forever on the verge of collapsing into chaos. Once the power figure is gone, so is the order.

The pure growth hierarchy is a utopian vision and one likely to tumble into chaos too. If no person or group is at the controls of the order, all of the inwardly directed people leveling up their skills will struggle to have their primal physiological needs met. Without a power structure in place making decisions to fortify the domains of the society—including a just system for all people to pursue their creative capacities without causing harm to others—the order will become unstable and collapse.

In his novel *The Threshing,* Tim Grahl made a choice of hierarchy that skews to the left of homeostatic. The power/dominance hierarchy is practically a tyranny at the start of the novel, but by the end, the very structure of society is a question mark, and chaos is a definite possibility.

To recap: The unbalanced setting and dueling hierarchies within that setting are the selective conventions of Action Story. These conventions give rise to internal conflicts within the protagonist and antagonist, or luminary agent and shadow agent. The result of those internal conflicts is the emergence of external conflicts in which the protagonist and antagonist apply their opposing agencies.

The constraints allow for life-like and believable internal conflict in the fictional characters that gives rise to their external action.

Action Story's selective constraint settings are the substance of its subgenres.

6

ACTION STORY'S FOUR SUBGENRES

The selective constraints of Action Story's setting can be divided into four sub-categories, each with four different dispositional qualities to further constrain the story environment. Again, selective constraints narrow the story's boundaries to home in on primal life–death conflicts.

1. Action Adventure or Human-Against-Nature Stories

These stories use unexpected events in the natural world or a specific setting or arena as the *force of conflict* or *shadow agent*, which we often call the *villain*. These stories can be further classified by four kinds of plot devices, or obvious hook attractors:

a. Labyrinth Plot: The object of desire is to save the *agency-deprived*, or what we often call the *victim(s)* and get out of a maze-like edifice. The movie *Die Hard* is a prime example.

b. Monster Plot: The shadow agent in this case is an animal or other living thing. *Jaws* is a prime example.

c. Environment Plot: The shadow agent is the actual global setting or environment. *Gravity* is a prime example.

d. Doomsday Plot: The victim deprived of agency in this case is the environment. The *luminary agent* or what we often call the protagonist (or hero or heroine in gendered terms) must save the environment from disaster. *Independence Day* is a prime example.

2. Action Epic or Human-Against-the State Stories

In these stories, the luminary agent must confront group-derived interpersonal conflict, societal institutions, or tyrants.

a. Rebellion Plot: The shadow agent is a visible tyrant, such as Darth Vader from *Star Wars*.

b. Conspiracy Plot: The shadow agent is an invisible tyrant. Examples include *Enemy of the State* and *The Bourne Identity*.

c. Vigilante Plot: A criminal organization serves as the shadow agent. *Above the Law* is a prime example.

d. Savior Plot: The shadow agent is someone who wants to destroy society or return it to pure chaos. *The Dark Knight* is a prime example.

3. Action Duel or Human-Against-Human Stories

In these stories, the luminary agent must confront direct and tightly defined interpersonal conflict, one person against another person.

a. Revenge Plot: The luminary agent chases the shadow agent. A prime example of this plot in the Western genre is *True Grit*.

b. Hunted Plot: The shadow agent chases the luminary agent. *The Fugitive* is a Thriller genre example of this plot.

c. Machiavellian Plot: The luminary agent sets two shadow agents against each other. For a Western genre example of this plot, see *A Fistful of Dollars*.

d. Collision Plot: The shadow agent sets two luminary agents against each other. The movie *Troy* is a prime example.

4. Action Clock or Human-Against-Time Stories

In these stories, time is the extra-personal force of conflict that serves as shadow agent.

a. Ransom Plot: The character embodying the role of shadow agent imposes a deadline. A prime example is *All the Money in the World*.

b. Countdown Plot: Natural circumstance serves as the shadow agent, imposing a deadline. *Armageddon* is a prime example.

c. Hold-out Plot: The luminary agent has to

hold out until others can rally. *The 300* is a prime example.

d. Fate Plot: Time serves as the shadow agent. A prime example is *Back to the Future.*

7

ACTION STORY'S ENABLING CONVENTIONS

Now that we have a handle on the selective constraints or conventions that narrow the Action Story problem, let's turn our attention to the **enabling constraints or conventions that give rise to possible solutions to the problem**.

Remember that selective constraints funnel the problem into a specific category, a need-based domain. And enabling constraints inside that particular domain give rise to the causes necessary to output effects.

Enabling constraints or conventions allow for life-like and believable internal conflict to surface within fictional characters. And that inner conflict then results in choices for behavioral action.

So, enabling conventions are the conditions that set up eventual payoff actions that emerge unexpectedly later on.

These unexpected events will be the key ingredient in creating a responsive conflict. All of these conflicts then give rise to a change in the life value in the scene (micro) and across the entire life–death range of Action Story (macro).

Another way to look at this is that enabling conventions make possible the causes that generate effects. The effects are the resulting events that answer the fundamental question posed by the genre. For Action Story, the fundamental question is "Will the luminary agent and the agency-deprived victim survive antagonism?" So, the following conventions of Action Story enable or set up the obligatory events that will provide an answer to that question.

Once the arena has been established, the next logical step for writer of Action Story is to clearly define a trinity of character roles across all of the nested units of story. The audience needs to know which character is playing each of these three roles in every beat, scene, sequence, act, subplot, and in the global story, so we need to assign these roles with care.

The good news is that we writers intuitively understand these roles. And the majority of the time, we put them in our story units unconsciously. So, it's not necessary to overthink these roles once you've figured out their representations. But later on, in the editing stage, it's a good idea to double-check to make sure each is clearly defined.

So, what are these must-have roles?

Consider the world in which we live as our global arena. Inside that global arena are specific domains (home, work, education, etc.) —a bunch of circles inside a vast circle.

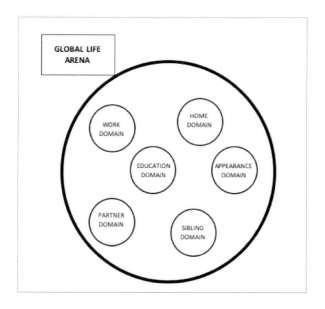

A human being's arena is the way they live or the totality of their physical and metaphysical experience, explicitly represented by one of those domains. It's what they sense physically, how they process those senses metaphysically inside their unconscious and conscious minds, and how they act upon the fallout from the unconscious and conscious processing is a fancy way of describing how we live.

What can happen, and often does, is that what we think is real can be severely misaligned with what's actually happening. We misread signs and signals and have difficulty conforming to our life's greater truth. So, to align ourselves better with reality, we have to change the way we process signs and signals. This isn't very easy to do, hence our need for stories on which to model our behavior.

The global life arena has a whole slew of specific domains embedded within it, and what's pictured above is just a small sampling. And as you'd expect, the genres themselves live inside each of our arenas as they concern how we acquire what we want and need to keep us stable.

A single person inside of their arena is an **agent.**

And their choices, or the processing-plus-action system they have to respond to the ever-changing physical and metaphysical environment of their particular arena, is **their agency.**

So, **agents have agency** (the ability to choose and act on those choices) **that they** apply inside their arena in response to unexpected events that change that arena.

In Action Story (indeed in all stories), there are three must-have players inside the story's selectively constrained arena.

ACTION STORY'S CONVENTIONAL CAST OF CHARACTERS

Role Number One:
The Luminary Agent
Protagonist/Heroine/Hero

Traditionally, this role has been referred to as the *hero* or *heroine*. In our quest to merge storytelling with the cognitive science realm, however, Story Grid proposes another term. It's a more abstract one that can rise above gender associations from story grammars of the past, which we think unnecessarily emphasize people's differences rather than their similarities.

The central figure of Action Story, which is usually the protagonist, is an agent that responds to the threat of death by applying their agency in the service of illuminating a path for the greatest common good. So, in our conception, the luminary agent is a figure who casts light into the darkness.

We define the *greatest common good* as the

path that allows the highest number of agents to survive and thrive, applying their agency to create a meaningful future. A meaningful future in the context of Action Story is one in which agents (characters) explore and organize cause-and-effect technologies out of the complexities of the unknown for the benefit of the ecosystem.

Role Number Two:
The Shadow Agent
Antagonist/Villain/Villainess

The shadow agent is usually the antagonist of Action Story. We associate this agent with darkness because we define dystopic existence as one where people are deprived of agency. When human beings are deprived of their agency, they are unable to create anything out of their embedded internal potential.

Not to get too philosophical about it, but one of Martin Heidegger's foundational ideas is that we humans lack a clearly defined human universal *essence*. What this means is that we can't be categorized into Platonic and Aristotelian ideas such as "living things that fly" or "living things that live in the water." In other words, human existence can't be reduced to a simple identifying statement.

And by extension, because we can't be put

into one single box, we must continuously strive to explore our *becoming*. Climbing the growth hierarchy is the only way for us as individuals to get closer to figuring out our particular essence, to *self-actualize*. As we do, the answers to those big questions of who we are and why we're here crystalize.

So, if we are deprived of our ability to pursue that striving to *become*, we will never know who we are or why we are here. That, for us at Story Grid, is darkness incarnate.

We succumb to darkness when we are forced or coerced, or even willingly choose, to turn over our agency to a shadow agent. When we hand over our ability to *become* or self-actualize to an external or internal force, we lose our ability to discover who we are and what we're supposed to be doing here.

The shadow agent is the role in a story that deprives other human beings of their agency, either through force, coercion, or charismatic persuasion. In contrast, the luminary agent opposes the deprivation of agency. So, naturally, these two forces conflict.

Role Number Three:
The Agency-Deprived/Victim

The agency-deprived, which is commonly known as the victim, is a character or group of characters in Action Story who have lost their ability to initiate, execute, and control their actions in the world. The domains in which they lose their agency are reflected in the selecting constraints of the subgenres.

In human-against-nature stories (Adventure), the power of the natural world emerges to rob us of our ability to apply our agency. A hurricane, a drought, a fire, or an avalanche, these can all cut us off from the rest of the world and deprive us of primal physiological needs. And as those needs remain unfulfilled, we slowly lose our agency, until someone, or a group of people, has the necessary insights to save us from death.

In human-against-the state stories (Epic), the power of social institutions can coerce or rob us of our ability to apply our agency. You'll see in Tim Grahl's *The Threshing* that his Action subgenres become progressively more complicated. The environment in his story initially constrains human beings in its ecosystem to adapt. They then must create artificial environments within the global environment to survive.

But to maintain control over the systems, these virtual environments have to level up their attraction. And soon the people in the story reach a place where they've turned over their agency to an addictive technology created by unseen human forces far away. Thus, the story shifts from one of human-against-nature (Adventure) to one of human-against-the-state (Epic). You'll discover many of these sorts of shifting subgenre moves in a lot of action stories.

In human-against-human stories (Duel), the luminary agent identifies the single source of agency-deprivation and they focus on defeating that figure or force. You'll see this rise of the story within *The Threshing* too.

Lastly, in human-against-time stories (Clock), the luminary discovers that their time to release the agency-deprived victim from captivity is limited. Thus, the urgency to act takes center stage. As you might expect, time also plays a role in *The Threshing*.

ACTION'S ENABLING CATALYSTS

The Speech in Praise of the Shadow Agent/Villain

HOW DOES a storyteller establish these destabilized environments and dueling hierarchies? How do they make clear to the audience these extraordinary abstract story structures at play?

This is where convention catalysts come in.

Thankfully, Action Story has just the thing to tell the audience what lies at the heart of the conflict. It's called the *speech in praise of the villain*, or as we Story Gridders call it now, *the speech in praise of the shadow agent*.

We're all very familiar with this convention. There's the moment in all action stories when someone discusses just how powerful and brilliant the opposing force is. The shadow agent could lay out their philosophy and thinking process, or one of the players opposing the shadow agent could explain what the luminary agent faces. Either way, Action Story requires this convention so that the audience can understand just how difficult the task is for those trying to overcome antagonism.

The speech in praise of the shadow agent defines the large power gap between the protagonist and the antagonist, which is an enabling constraint that forces the luminary agent to grow and level up their skills and worldview.

The Deadline

Another excellent tool to set up intensity of conflict is time pressure, which accelerates the series of choices the players must make and enact. The *deadline* is an enabling convention of Action Story. Consider the following examples:

- There is only so much air left in the chamber where the agency-deprived victim is being held.
- A bomb will detonate if the luminary agent does not comply with the demands of the shadow agent.
- If the speed of the bus dips below 35 miles per hour, it will explode.

Clocks pump up tension and stress in the players within the story and, by extension, they evoke excitement in the audience. This sets up the active payoffs later on with intensity.

Set-Piece Action Sequences

We are all very familiar with these conventions. Imagine a big chase sequence where the luminary agent barely escapes the clutches of the shadow agent. Or a heist sequence where a character must take a valuable resource from someone or something else to move forward in their mission to rescue the agency-deprived. These mini-action stories within the global story are essential to set up the payoffs later on.

Not only do these sequences entertain in the moment of experience, they also illustrate the luminary agent's worldview in such a way that they reveal strengths and weaknesses. The skilled storyteller will show how the luminary agent births new skills in these set pieces. That is, they learn a new skill or technique inadvertently in these sequences that they will insightfully activate to solve a more significant problem later on. Patricia Highsmith was a master at employing this technique in her Tom Ripley novels. (Ripley, of course, is both a shadow agent and a luminary agent in one, one of the first postmodern anti-heroes.)

Conventions for Action Story constrain a storyteller's choices, which in turn allows for the emergence of innovation inside the genre. Without constraints, storytelling would be incoherent. Embrace the conventions (selective and enabling) as the means to limit the search space of your imagination, and innovate within those boundaries. Knowing what needs to be established for Action Story will laser focus your ability to try new solutions to solve age-old story problems insightfully.

8

ACTION STORY'S OBLIGATORY EVENTS

Conventions set up conflicts. And from conflicts come changes in value from scene to scene and across the entire Action Story arc.

But where and when do these conflicts take place in the context of the story? How do they unfold, and how can you create the cause and effect pattern that a reader of Action Story will recognize?

The answer comes in the form of obligatory events. When the selective and enabling constraints or conventions of Action Story are adhered to, certain events tend to emerge organically.

What follows is a list of twenty events in Action Story that align with the Five Commandments of Storytelling. Five scenes represent the Inciting Incident, the Turning Point Progressive Complication, the Crisis, the Climax, and the Resolution for each of our four

Story Grid global components. In other words, these five scenes appear in the Beginning Hook, Middle Build One, Middle Build Two, and Ending Payoff. These scenes are vessels that contain the obligatory events for Action Story.

Keep in mind that after you create these events, you can revise and rearrange them inside a global framework that is not linear. A story such as *Pulp Fiction* is a perfect example of a rejiggering of events in nonlinear form. You'll also discover that many of these events can be whittled down to moments in a scene or manipulated in unique and potent ways. They might even occur "off stage." What a writer must know, though, is precisely how each event is represented in their work.

Remember that these obligatory events in your story are the payoff moments that your genre's most dedicated fans expect; they are experts in picking out the most powerful events of the work. Ignore these moments at your peril. But you also won't satisfy genre readers by repeating the same old version of the events. So, while it may be challenging to freshen and innovate these events in Action Story, you must do so to write a story that lasts longer than you.

Beginning Hook (approximately 25 percent of the Story)

1. The Inciting Incident: Attack

The global and beginning hook inciting incident of Action Story must have an embedded agency-depriving and life-threatening attack by the forces of antagonism. This attack can be on a single character or a group of characters, but it must have a profound life-destabilizing effect for your protagonist and luminary agent.

The unexpected attack (phere) can be causal (a purposeful action by an antagonist) or coincidental (a non-human antagonistic force, such as a wild animal or a significant weather event).

At first, the protagonist fails to register the need to respond to this attack or chooses to avoid engagement because they are focused on a different goal. They assume the attack is someone else's problem and make the minimum effort necessary, skirting responsibility.

This is the protagonist's first stage of processing the fear arising from the unexpected event. They freeze and behave as if everything is as it has always been and use the same goal-oriented behavior to evaluate their circumstances. The protagonist is inattentive to the reality that their ordered life has been disturbed by the phere event and that they are now living in a confusing and disordered system.

2. The Turning Point Progressive Complication of the Beginning Hook: Sensing Disorder

The protagonist's inattention to the antagonistic force builds until such time as their life value or that of others turns dangerously closer to or tips into death.

This turning point is the result of one of two events. The antagonist may attack again. Or, the protagonist receives more revelatory information about the earlier unexpected event(s) such that they begin to recognize and *make sense* of the disordered nature of the system. Either way, the protagonist realizes the forces of antagonism are life-threatening to themselves and others.

3. The Crisis of the Beginning Hook: Running Away to Reluctant Engagement

The crisis question of the beginning hook is when the protagonist finally *understands the meaning* of the sense they make of their disordered state. It means they face a best bad choice or irreconcilable goods decision. They must decide whether to look out for number one and evade the antagonistic force to continue pursuing their ego-derived goal or to engage with the antagonism and take up the mission to restore order for those deprived of their agency.

4. The Climax of the Beginning Hook: Agreeing to Fight

The climax of the beginning hook results in the reluctant protagonist agreeing to engage with the antagonistic force. The protagonist realizes their refusal to fight deprives not only their own agency but also that of others, and so they are responsible for the suffering of others. The resulting internal torment is untenable for the protagonist. They agree to engage, deciding that the only real option is to confront the threat.

The fear response to the unexpected attack of the beginning hook—freeze, flight, and then reluctantly fight—pushes the protagonist into engaging with the unknown.

5. The Resolution of the Beginning Hook: The Fix it and Forget it Mission

The beginning hook resolves with the protagonist agreeing to engage the antagonist with a pre-programmed strategy using the minimum effort necessary to restore order. Their ego misdirects them into thinking they have the necessary capabilities already in hand to achieve this goal.

Middle Build One (approximately 25 percent of the Story)

6. The Inciting Incident of Middle Build One: A Whole New World

The inciting incident of the middle build makes clear the liminal shift from the protagonist's old, familiar environment introduced in the beginning hook to an unknown, new environment.

The protagonist must adapt and excel in this environment to cause the effect they desire (usually to restore balance), but they make the mistake of assuming their usual bag of tricks will be sufficient. The protagonist wants to get back to normal as quickly as possible, so their confrontation with an entirely new environment (another big unexpected phere event) disorients them.

Here, the protagonist meets the threshold guardian, an archetypical figure who marks the boundary between worlds and indoctrinates them into this new one.

7. The Turning Point Progressive Complication of Middle Build One: The Protagonist Becomes the Target of the Antagonist

It is here that the protagonist comes "into the sights" of the antagonist or forces of antagonism and is thus closer to death. The protagonist meets a challenge and must outmaneuver the antagonist in some way, and they either successfully thwart the antagonist's agenda or not. Regardless of their success in the event, the protagonist demonstrates extraordinary ability to "shine through" in the challenge.

The antagonist (or indifferent force of antagonism) recognizes a formidable agency when they see it, and resolves to engage the protagonist. If the antagonist is human, they target the protagonist. If the antagonist is indifferent (for example a monster or the environment), the protagonist has made themselves environmentally vulnerable. That is, they are now exposed to more significant effects from the forces of antagonism than before. They are on a cliff face.

Unlike the protagonist, the antagonist is not disoriented or confused about how to apply their agency in this environment. Antagonists have tremendous confidence in their abilities and power and have trained themselves to attack unexpected events as soon as they arise. It is for this reason that we often say the middle build of a story is "owned by the villain."

It may be helpful to think of the protagonist as the big unexpected event (the phere) that drops into the life of the antagonist. The antagonist must destroy the protagonist, coerce them into following their commands, or risk not attaining their goal.

Because of their developing powers, the

protagonist finds themselves alienated from the rest of their social class and must contend with enemies within the group they've been tasked to aid, while they also cultivate allies. They are vulnerable to shapeshifters, covert agents loyal to the antagonist, or independent agents playing personal and hidden goal-oriented games.

The protagonist's life is further destabilized at the turning point, but they think if they can hold out, their skills will see them through and get them back to normal.

8. The Crisis of Middle Build One: Should I Comply or Defy?

How the protagonist makes sense of the antagonist or vice versa raises a meaningful crisis question: "Do I work with this agent, or do I oppose this agent's plan?"

Considering the crisis of middle build one from the antagonist's point of view can be extremely helpful. The antagonist is always looking for powerful agents to use as tools.

The antagonist may respond to the protagonist's abilities by attacking or attempting to coerce them. This crisis event either gives the protagonist a false sense of security (closer to life if the antagonist is recruiting them) or sobers them up in such a way that they understand just how difficult their task is (closer to death if they are attacked again).

9. The Climax of Middle Build One: The Shadow Agent Asserts Their Dominant Power

In the climax event of middle build one, the antagonist actively asserts their power in response to the protagonist's decision to oppose them, or even if they join them. It is such a monstrous execution of force that the protagonist's behavioral toolkit fails.

The protagonist is overwhelmed and responds in a way that the antagonist does not anticipate.

10. The Resolution of Middle Build One: No Way Out, The Point of No Return

The resolution of middle build one is the irreversible change event of the global story. The protagonist's response to their fall into chaos causes the entire system to become chaotic too. The antagonist and all those in the environment find themselves unhinged by the protagonist's reaction.

Chaos is the experience of not knowing what to do or even what is going on, with no knowledge of how to contend with random unexpected events. The world is unconstrained.

All the tools the protagonist has used before to gain power against the rest of society completely fail (or so they think). The antagonist and the rest of the figures in the story don't know what's going on either.

This moment in Action Story is often referred to as the midpoint climax, but it is structurally the resolution event of middle build one. The protagonist discovers they will never get back to normal. Their fix-it-and-forget-it mission is impossible, and their skills and plans are inadequate to deal with the reality of the challenges they face.

This is the moment when your audience will lock into the story and wonder how it is going to end. The trick to this event is to let it run without offering any solutions. The rest of the middle build (middle build two) is all about how the protagonist will climb out of this chaotic situation.

Middle Build Two (approximately 25 percent of the Story)

II. The Inciting Incident of Middle Build Two: An Encounter with an Unexplained Event (the Noumenal)

The protagonist experiences a mysterious encounter with an unexplainable event. Something happens to the protagonist that can be a positive or negative development, but is random and transformational.

This experience is symbolic of the *noumenal* realm, popularized by philosopher

Immanuel Kant. The noumenal is all that we are incapable of explaining or knowing. It is counterbalanced by the *phenomenal*, which are knowable patterns (what we sense but have not fully defined or examined definitively) that can be converted into cause-and-effect procedures.

A clear example of the encounter with the noumenal is the use of the glowing suitcase in *Pulp Fiction*.

The protagonist and the antagonist contend with the unexplained event in ways that counterbalance each other's response. The protagonist makes an active choice to accept the disorientation of chaos, the lack of pattern, and constraints. Once the protagonist accepts that they can't know everything, they learn to respond to phere events with more flexibility. They take the unexpected events moment-by-moment without a fixed strategy to exploit or destroy them.

The antagonist reacts to unexplained events differently. They believe that their intellect and worldview are so perfectly conceived, rational, logical, and ordered that they can control anything, including the unexpected.

12. **The Turning Point Progressive Complication of Middle Build Two: All is Lost**

The protagonist comes out of their

noumenal experience and begins to explore the world in a new way. Instead of pre-programed plans, they begin to pay attention to unexpected events as they arise. Still, because this is a new behavioral system, it emerges imperfectly. The protagonist then suffers a significant set-back, which turns the value to the inevitability of death.

Death is now a certainty. Someone is going to die (make sure someone does) because everyone dies. Death is the fundamental existential problem and the substance of Action Story. So, the value shifts at this turning point from life to death.

The protagonist despairs that all is lost. They don't know how to proceed now that death is certain.

13. The Global and Middle Build Two Crisis: How can my death be meaningful?

Middle build two is when the global crisis of the story emerges—what is the best way to live if we're going to die?

The protagonist must decide, now that death is imminent, what they can do to make their life meaningful. How can they contribute to the collective knowledge of their entire species before they leave Earth?

If the protagonist saves only themselves in this dark situation, others will suffer. This is what we at Story Grid call an *irreconcilable goods* crisis. What's good for the protagonist is bad for everyone else. So, as the protagonist realizes that they are eventually going to die anyway, they must decide whether to selfishly put their wants and needs above those of others or sacrifice themselves for the greater good.

Here, Action Story gets right to the heart of this life-and-death conundrum.

The antagonist, though, does not face these existential dilemmas. The antagonist sees themselves as above the crowd, with a responsibility to do what it takes to remain alive. They justify that selfishness as the means to *serve the greater good*. They reason that the world needs leaders, not martyrs. And they make very compelling cases for their ideology.

The crisis event of middle build two is also the global crisis. Do I save myself, or do I sacrifice myself to serve the greater good?

14. The Middle Build Two Climax: Absolute Commitment

The protagonist decides to confront the antagonist and release the agency-deprived victim from their power. No matter what.

The critical element for this event is that the protagonist acts willingly and with the courage to engage with the antagonist's powerful algorithms (definitive tactics), using only their reasonable heuristics (rules of thumb) to defend themselves and their allies.

15. Resolution of Middle Build Two: Preparations to Enter the Ultimate Arena

Middle build two resolves as the protagonist begins to prepare with great humility for their big fight with the super-powerful antagonist. They will fight to save the victim even though they are likely to die in the process. They commit to making meaningful choices and act with as little noise in their heads as they possibly can by getting in the arena of the antagonist and applying all their capacities.

They say goodbye to their loved ones. Last suppers are held.

The protagonist has now climbed up and out of chaos and is prepared for the complexity of the natural world and the showdown with the antagonist.

The Ending Payoff (approximately 25 percent of the Story)

16. The Inciting Incident of the Ending Payoff: No Holds Barred

In the inciting incident of the ending payoff, the protagonist enters the sanctum of the antagonist. This event requires a leveling up of the spectacle so that the stakes and balance of power are precise and asymmetrical.

With a definite home-field advantage, the antagonist hits the protagonist with serious firepower from the outset. A big life-threatening phere drops in to kick off the final push of the story. The phere should *mirror* the beginning hook of the story; that is, the phere should be in the same category as the global inciting incident, but at a much higher level.

The point of this mirroring effect is to highlight the change in the protagonist from the beginning of the story to the end. They dealt with the initial phere by using their typical behavior, which was insufficient and which led to the reanimation of this same phere in the ending payoff with a much higher level of power.

The protagonist comes to understand that it will take more than one mind to defeat such a powerful force. The entire ending payoff will demonstrate participatory knowledge cultivation. The protagonist listens to and relies upon others (as they never have before) in this final quadrant of the story.

17. The Turning Point Progressive Complication of the Ending Payoff: Someone the Audience Cares About Dies

The turning point progressive complication of the ending payoff of Action Story requires *a literal shift into death*.

To bring storytelling's cathartic effects

embedded within Action Story into full play, an experience of loss is required. We need to see that the stakes are life and death. A character or characters that the audience cares about must die to escalate the stakes for the protagonist. They aren't just fighting to define the meaning of their own life anymore but for their allies' lives too.

18. The Ending Payoff Crisis: Do the Ends Justify the Means?

The protagonist must face a best bad choice or irreconcilable goods decision. Is their mission more important than the life or agency of a single person? Do the ends justify the means? Are they willing to let an individual die in order to save a whole group of the agency-deprived?

Can the protagonist generate insight at this moment that does not betray the sanctity of the individual to save the group?

This crisis is a crucial choice for the protagonist. Of course, the antagonist has no problem sacrificing anyone to their mission. Hence, these moments can also turn on the actions of a shapeshifter, in other words, unexpected responses from figures the audience does not anticipate will be on the same team as the protagonist.

19. The Ending Payoff Climax: The Protagonist at the Mercy of the Antagonist

This is the global climax of the story, as well as the climax of the ending payoff. This is the *core event* of Action Story, the moment by which audiences will come to judge the storyteller. In other words, it's the big moment that must be satisfying to your audience in order for your story to work. You can do everything right throughout the story, but if you fail to make this event surprising, you will disappoint your audience.

The protagonist is plunged into a seemingly inescapable, unsolvable conundrum. The antagonist has them dead to rights and will undoubtedly enjoy their suffering and death. Remember, the antagonist has been irritated, challenged, and tormented by the protagonist since the point of no return. Now, at last, they can rid themselves of this menace.

The trick to figuring out how the protagonist can escape this situation is to have them defeat the antagonist by 1) physically overpowering them, 2) outwitting them, or 3) a combination of these.

The protagonist will succeed because they adapt an old skill or a new skill emerges.

20. The Resolution of the Ending Payoff and Global Story: The Reward

The protagonist either defeats the antagonist or sacrifices themselves in such a way that the antagonist will be destroyed or face innumerable challenges from other adversaries in the future. The protagonist is rewarded for their efforts either externally (a big thank-you parade, etc.) or internally (martyrdom in the service of the greater good).

9

WRITING ACTION STORY

Our abstract representations of the obligatory events of Action Story represent the fundamental on-the-ground form for all stories. Remember that form constrains your choices, and understanding the substance of form will free you from confusion. That is the indispensable heuristic for a storyteller.

Action Story is made up of a wonderfully compelling series of choices (intentional solutions to a set of story problems) that the creator must confront and resolve. The higher the resolution of knowledge you have about each component of the greater whole of the form, the better your ability to directly engage with every formal decision with serious intent. We at Story Grid remain committed to exploring story form so that you can bring your best storytelling self to the fore.

We submit that Action Story is the primal

evolutionary genre, the first story form, and the one from which all others have evolved. With the understanding of Action Story's value and the options available to you to embed and express a meaningful controlling idea, as well as the conventions and obligatory events that make for a compelling action narrative, you now have a much richer understanding of how to solve the global Action Story creation problem.

While we've been conditioned to believe that action stories aren't deep or meaningful, that they are "just entertainment," they have emerged as the most important stories ever told. They saved lives thousands of years ago, and continue to do so today.

We can't stress this enough: embracing the primacy of action is a storytelling necessity.

A brush with death changes lives, and Action Story gives us an encounter with that inevitable safely. At its best, Action Story prescribes a way for us to live meaningful lives while also cautioning us how to detect and defuse those among us who wish to tilt the world to their will, depriving others of their agency.

We need great Action Story now more than ever.

10

STORY GRID TOOLS TO WORK THROUGH YOUR ACTION STORY

As you will have experienced reading through this guide, there are a number of elements for the aspiring Action Story writer to understand and integrate into their work. We at Story Grid have three global strategic tools to keep all of these concepts in mind and at hand throughout your writing process.

They are:

I. The Story Grid Global Foolscap Page:

This tool allows you to track the development of your entire story on one sheet of paper. Visit https://storygrid.com/contender/threshing/ to learn more and to see an example of just how this macro outline is put together.

II. The Story Grid Spreadsheet:

This tool allows you to track the scene-by-scene progression of your entire story. Visit https://storygrid.com/contender/threshing/ to learn more about how to use a spreadsheet to track the micro movements of your work as well as the continuity of your story.

III. The Story Grid Infographic:

This tool is the culmination of your final work. Visit https://storygrid.com/contender/threshing/ to learn more. The infographic uses both the macro overview of the Story Grid Global Foolscap Page and the micro scene-by-scene progression of your story to create a graphical representation of how well your story 'moves.' That is, it allows you to see how your potential readers/listeners/viewers will experience the work on an emotional level.

ABOUT THE AUTHOR

SHAWN COYNE created, developed, and expanded the story analysis and problem-solving methodology the Story Grid during his quarter-century-plus career in book publishing. A seasoned story editor, book publisher, and ghostwriter, Coyne has also co-authored *The Ones Who Hit the Hardest: The Steelers, the Cowboys, the '70s, and the Fight For America's Soul* with Chad Millman and *Cognitive Dominance: A Brain Surgeon's Quest to Out-Think Fear* with Mark McLaughlin, M.D. With his friend and editorial client Steven Pressfield, Coyne runs Black Irish Entertainment, LLC, publisher of the cult classic book *The War of Art.* Coyne oversees the Story Grid Universe, LLC, which includes Story Grid University and Story Grid Publishing, with his friend and editorial client Tim Grahl.

Made in United States
North Haven, CT
26 January 2023

31681026R00062